P
REINVESTING ... YOUR RHETORIC

"The OCD Presentation Method is a roadmap to effective communication for all stages of leadership, and we have found it to be an outstanding toolkit that can be referred back to over and over again. This has proven to be especially beneficial in remote working environments, allowing our teams to connect quickly with both internal and external stakeholders, and to keep them meaningfully engaged. Everyone can benefit from this."

— **Eric Gillespie**, Govini Founder and Chairman

"My experience delivering speeches and presenting both personally and professionally are extensive. I've been asked to deliver sermons in a religious setting to spark belief and in the workplace to motivate people into action. Therefore, I perform well on the delivery aspect of public speaking. In Jill's course at Harvard, she taught our cohort of seasoned professionals and executives a framework of organize, content, and delivery (OCD) which provided much needed structure on how I prepare for a speech and arrange my content to more accurately fit the audience's expectations. Working on these initial steps provided a process I can engage in to ensure consistency in my approach which augments my ability to deliver and serve my audience's needs. I am a better communicator for it!"

—**John Maurelus**, Banking Executive

"OCD has changed the way I deliver speeches. It gives me a clear method to follow and never fails me."

—**Julie Lalwani**, Financial Advisor, Edward Jones

"After thirty plus years in industry I had the reputation of being a pretty good public speaker, but in hindsight I suspect that my speeches were mechanized and perhaps a bit sterile. Jill's taught me how to lead with my heart and in the process transformed how I thought about preparing and delivering a speech. As a result, she made me both more effective in my public remarks and more efficient in preparation. Her coaching opened a wealth of new perspectives for me to work from. I will be forever grateful to her for pushing me where I had never had the courage to go on my own."

—**Don Parker**, Retired Executive Manager from the financial services industry

Reinvesting In Your Rhetoric

Reinvesting In Your Rhetoric

Establish a **meaningful** connection with **any** audience.

Based on the OCD Presentation Method™

Jill Slye

Deeds Publishing | Athens

Published by Deeds Publishing in Athens, GA
www.deedspublishing.com

Printed in The United States of America

Cover design by Mark Babcock.

ISBN 978-1-950794-24-9

Books are available in quantity for promotional or premium use.
For information, email info@deedspublishing.com.

First Edition, 2020

10 9 8 7 6 5 4 3 2 1

This book is dedicated to all of my past, present and future students, clients, and Professional Development Program participants.

To my past students for allowing me the opportunity to build and shape this method; my future students who will provide me the opportunity to learn and grow; and to all, for giving me the opportunity to watch you change the world, one speech at a time.

In loving memory of my Granny, Blanche Abruzese.

Contents

Acknowledgements

First to my loving parents who helped shape the woman I am today. Mom and Dad, you provided the life lessons, love, support, and encouragement that allowed me to find my voice.

To my entire family, with whom I shared many adventures from selling trucks to family vacations. Each of you played a special role in helping me find my inner passions and goals.

My loving husband, whose love and support were my lifeline. My incredible son who shared me with a computer for the last year. He did a fantastic job posing for the pictures in this book, and his humor and hugs got me through each and every chapter.

I love you all and my heart is filled with gratitude.

To my Aunt Nat who read and edited each and every sentence of this book, and amazed me with her dedication to my success of completing it. Uncle Bob's introduction to Bob Babcock and the team at Deeds Publishing was a life changer. Christina Sookhoo filled multiple shoes of editor, researcher, production assistant, and teaching assistant, and most of all my personal cheerleader. Sarah Anne Stinnett kept me smiling through multiple semesters, and I will always cherish our time working together.

Bob Cohen encouraged me to never give up on myself and rooted for me long after I told him I wanted to be an author in 2005! Marjorie North unlocked my potential by seeing in me what I could not see in myself. Suzanne Spreadbury and her team welcomed me into the Harvard Extension School with open arms. I was fortunate that Mark Ochida, Lynn Rublee, Linda Spencer, Stephen Blinn, and Anne Write embraced my words, "I am never leaving".

Alex Bandow, Mike Davis, Gregory Aimo, Kerry Folley, Joanna Do, and Ethan Contini-Field supported my goals to shift to an online curriculum, and just in time!

To my dearest friends Sherry Fraser, Mary Ellen Stevenson, Amy Bannister, Terry Eagan, (87), Paula Callari, Brenda Field, and Amy Trupe whose love and support carried me through the ups and downs of life.

Thanks to the Havard Extension School Professional Development team and Dr. Sang Park from the Harvard School of Dental Medicine for providing me with the platform to reach more professionals with my method.

Additionally, I want to thank the guests of my new

Podcast Series, Josh Shipp, Rachel Trudel, Dathan Lumpkins, Denise Freimouth, Harry Simmons, Valerie O'Kane, and Louis Mitchell, who helped soft launch the book, and provided their support of what I teach.

Finally, a double thanks to my best friend, the love of my life, husband, guiding light, and biggest supporter, my husband David Slye.

1
29 Years of Investing

Introducing Communication

In early 1991, if you asked me to meet you in a restaurant for dinner, I would promptly tell you that you needed to meet me outside of the restaurant, NOT inside. I couldn't dare go in by myself and find you. My fear, doubt, and insecurity got in the way of most social activities.

After the summer of '91, all of that changed. I was handed a stack of business cards with my name printed on them, and I was told to go out and 'pound the pavement.' My father's commercial truck dealership was one of the few in regional New York at that time that required truck salesmen to go out and cold call for new customers. I was a shy and insecure 20-year-old female suddenly faced with figuring out how to sell trucks and overcome the fear of public speaking. Off I went, one of three women in the entire United States selling commercial trucks. I began selling Isuzu and Freight-liner trucks in New York, New Jersey, and Connecticut, which included all five New York boroughs.

The temperature began to drop as we approached fall in New York City. I would hide my black clunky boots under a floor length skirt, while a hefty sweater kept me warm. Cautiously, I entered the open garage doors on West 8th Avenue in the heart of the west side of Manhattan. This neighborhood was known as 'the meat market,' long before it became known as to-day's chic part of town. There was an odor that turned my stomach. It was a mix of blood and sanitizing floor cleaner. The blood left a metallic taste in my mouth while the chlorine stung my nose. It was a cross be-tween the smell of a hospital, and a murder scene. The floors rippled with water flowing from the back room and there was a sound screaming from the forced water coming from the power-washer hosing down the large hooks and bloody floor where dozens of 75lb slabs of meat hung before they were loaded on a truck to go out to some of the finest restaurants in Manhattan and the five boroughs.

I spotted a couple of men wearing white coats with blue gloves, but then my glasses fogged up from the mist of water wafting off the floor. I yelled over the power washer, "HI, CAN I PLEASE TALK TO THE PERSON WHO IS IN CHARGE OF PURCHAS-ING YOUR TRUCKS?" I was directed into a small

5'x7'crammed office. I introduced myself and began asking my prepared sixteen sales questions.

This was the beginning of a 17-year career in the commercial truck industry. So, you ask, how did I get here now, writing about how to become a more effective communicator? Let's start with this:

It was 1991 in Yonkers, NY, I had newly dropped out of college and went to work in a male-dominated industry in my family's third generation medium and heavy-duty truck dealership. I was filled with fear, doubt, and insecurity! But, boy, did I learn a lot of lessons in communication during those 17 years; not necessarily the same communication I now use at Harvard University, but lots of lessons (those stories are for another book).

Fast forward 28 years. Today I am blessed to work with people from around the world and every day it is my goal to positively impact their lives. Everyone I work with has their own individual personal goals to improve their communication style, and I provide them with a set of tools to achieve those objectives. I push, cheer, and encourage everyone I work with to step way outside of their comfort zone. I ask them to never stop the process of striving to become a more effective communicator. I have watched students and clients go on to make TV appearances, record TedTalks, become closer to family members, find new jobs, start their own business, and make positive changes in the world...one presentation at a time!

This book is an overview of how to use a new lens to look at your communication style and identify your strengths and areas for improvement. Like any pair of glasses, the framework in this book has two lenses. We use the first lens to look at our communication style, and then we shift to the second lens to look at our communication partner. We then identify what works, and what does not work well. This takes time and patience. As with any investment, there are upturns and downturns in the market, but in the long term it pays off. It is crucial to trust that this process can be applied over a lifetime. As I tell all of my students, "Take what you need and leave the rest."

My most successful students have made small adjustments that have provided life-changing effects. You will get out of this what you put into it! Let us begin our journey. Let's look at who we are going to entrust with our new investment.

2
Making the Investment

Who are you going to entrust with your new invest-ment?

The answer to that question is...yourself! In most cases, investments are made for the long term with hopes of a positive return, and we don't check them multiple times a day. We set up the investment as best we can, making adjustments as needed, and then wait for it to grow exponentially. Similarly, we spend years establishing our communication style and don't look back. We don't take the time to check on our investment because we trust that over a long period of time it will continue to grow, except when we hear the market dip or spike. Similar to public speaking, it is only when we are asked to give a presentation or speak up in a meeting that we dip and spike and go into panic mode or start to worry about putting together a presentation.

Let's put on a new lens and begin to reinvest in

OUR communication style, in order to eliminate much of the work, energy, and panic that goes into professional presenting. Our new lens will bring an advanced awareness and reveal areas for improvement, and more importantly, will reveal our strengths. It is easy to get so caught up in what we need to improve that we often forget to identify our natural talents and build upon that prowess as well. Before we adopt this new lens, we need to acknowledge one of the biggest obstacles of speaking publicly: nerves.

Addressing Your NERVES

Addressing nerves and the fear of public speaking is always the starting point of any class I teach, or conversation I have regarding public speaking. FEAR is the largest barrier between a speaker and his/her audience. How do we overcome this giant obstacle? While I don't have the cure, I do have an analogy that may help you better understand how to deal with your body's reaction to public speaking. Also, by showing you how to reinvest in your communication style, this book will provide simple suggestions, tools, and techniques for improving your communication on multiple levels, which will ultimately lead to confidence and a reduction of that fear.

REINVESTING IN YOUR RHETORIC

Tad Simons' "Scared Speechless: Understanding and Conquering Stage Fright" unpacks the fear of public speaking. Anxiety associated with public speaking, when a sea of eyes are looking at you, is simply your body's 'fight or flight' survival response. In "Scared Speechless," the fear behind public speaking is thought to stem from individualistic experiences or cultures. Understanding and establishing what is behind your fear of public speaking is often the direct way to overcome fear. (2.1) For example, maybe you've always felt intimidated by large crowds, or had a previous bad experience publicly expressing yourself. Your fear is different from anyone else's and we can't address fear with a blanket statement. You have to understand where your fear comes from before you address it.

Once I found my voice and began teaching and working with clients, I drew a simple analogy demonstrating how I shifted from being an insecure, shy, introvert, into someone who enjoys getting up in front of an audience.

If you walk through a door and someone jumps out from behind the door and yells, "BOO", you will experience an involuntary physical reaction. Your reaction could include increased heart rate, sweaty palms, shaky limbs, and you may even let out a yell. Our amygdala is the part of the brain that stimulates fight or flight. This function of our brain gave us the ability to evolve as a society by reacting to anticipated danger. If you walk through that door again after being scared the first time, this time knowing the person is going to say 'BOO', chances are you will still have an involuntary reaction, but one that is not as severe as the first time. By the 10th time you walk through the door, it is a mere interruption in your step and no longer a scare.

Why? Because you have learned there is no immediate imposing danger, and have therefore moderated your reaction. The same can apply to public speaking. If we do it once, and acknowledge that our body has a reaction, then each time we speak publicly, it will become easier to accept our reaction, until it becomes a mere interruption in our step.

Take a minute to remember that Friday morning in fifth grade when, although two weeks ago, you knew you had that test, you decided NOT to study until the last minute. You walked into class and your palms were sweaty, your heart was racing, and all you wanted to do was run out of the room. Sound familiar? This is where the old saying, 'Proper Planning Prevents Poor Performance' would have come in handy! Why do we still wait until the last minute before preparing ourselves to give a speech?

Exercise: Take a minute to write down and acknowledge how your body reacts when you are in front of an audience:

_____

_____

_____

It is important to note that most of what we physically experience from nerves can't be seen by our audience. They are distracted by their own self-centered thoughts and ideas, otherwise known as WIIFM (What's In It For Me). When I am speaking and teach about nerves, I always ask the audience if they heard my heart beat, noticed my knees shaking, or heard my voice cracking. They always respond, "No." When I ask why, they say, "Because you have confidence and you have prepared." I reply, "Why, yes, I do have confidence in my message and I have prepared. However, I did still have all of the above occurring and, the only reason you did not notice them is because you were not looking for my nerves." And neither is your audience. An audience is usually tapped into the frequency of WIIFM. As a self-centered species, as the speaker we worry about how we deal with nervousness, while our audience is just as self-centered, and thinking about what they are going to get out of our presentations. In addition, the audience is so grateful it's YOU up there and not them. They are not looking at your knees!

Pocket Guide for a Successful Investment and Building Confidence

Effective communication embraces three aspects, which I call O.C.D.

Organization | Content | Delivery

Let's use our new lens and look at the basics of organizing a presentation. Whether we are speaking before two (2) or 2,000 people, we should still employ this foundation. Some of this may be familiar to you from taking previous public speaking courses, reading books, watching webinars, or reading articles. However, now that you are committed to reinvesting in your rhetoric, this information should begin to look a bit different. Investing is for the long haul, and this concept of OCD brings with it a newer, wider perspective. We are not just preparing for a one-time event. We are setting the foundation to reduce wasting time in the future, both our own and our audience's time. That may sound harsh, but there is too much competition for "air time" in our world, so we better be prepared to use our time wisely. After all, we are still people who have to communicate with people … At least for now.

3
Investing in Your Presentation

Organization: The "O" in O.C.D

How we organize a speech affects the outcome of how our message is received. When I teach Organization to my students and clients, I often ask, "Who has never used a GPS, map, or atlas when trying to get to an unknown destination?" I have yet to have anyone raise their hand. Our society needs, wants, and craves direction. We want to know where we are and where we are going. Every moment our brain creates memories based on experiences and yet, with all the internal and external interference, it is difficult to retain those memories without distortion. In order to have a lasting impact on our audience, we first need to understand how we organize our thoughts.

Let's give our new lens a test run with this first exercise:

Organize Your Thoughts

Instructions: Is it easy for you to put your ideas and thoughts in a logical order?

In the space provided, Create an Outline for a 3 Minute Speech about a success or failure that had great impact on your life.

_____

_____

_____

_____

_____

_____

_____

_____

_____

_____

_____

_____

_____

_____

_____

_____

_____

_____

_____

_____

_____

Determine Your Exercise Results:

If...you created a well-structured outline with a logical order using the proper outline format, including Roman numerals, upper case letters, Arabic numerals, lower case letters with indentation, then congratulations—you have strong organizational skills and the ability to quickly put your ideas and thoughts in order.

If...you wrote out full sentences and utilized less than half the page, then you are able to convey your thoughts and ideas, but are not entirely familiar with how to create a proper outline. You do however, have a solid concept of timing and flow.

If...you filled the entire page with full sentences, ran out of room, and found this exercise challenging, then this is not a bad thing but it could use some additional work. This chapter will demonstrate how to work from a well-structured outline derived from an organizational speech pattern, which will keep you on point and assist with your presentation, timing, and organization.

There is an example of an effective outline on the following page.

Sample Organization Outline
for Topical Pattern

I. Introduction
    A. Attention getter: get your audience on the edge of their seat
    B. Motivational Statement: tapping into your audience's WIIFM
    C. Credibility Statement: information about your "fire in the belly"
    D. Preview Statement: reiterates your main points as they are listed in the body of your speech

II. Main Point 1
    A. Sub-point
        1. Sub Sub-point
        2. Sub Sub-point
    B. Sub-point
        1. Sub Sub-point

III. Main Point 2
    A. Sub-point
    B. Sub-point
    C. Sub-point

IV. Main Point 3
    A. Sub-point
        1. Sub Sub-point

      2. Sub Sub-point

   B .Sub-point

      1. Sub Sub-point

V. Conclusion

   A. Review Statement: the same as your preview statement

   B. Repeat motivational statement. *Remind the audience of the benefits of your solution (if persuasive)*.

   C. Strong ending (creative, immediate, impactful, tangible)

Note: This may seem repetitive but this is the best starting point. Your audience will walk away remembering 30-45 seconds of your speech. Repeating and reviewing the material in your conclusion, in the same order it was presented in the speech, will help your main points stick with your audience.

An outline should have main points, sub points, additional sub sub points, and perhaps sub-sub-sub points, depending on the topic and length of the speech. Each line should have 4 words or less. While the reason behind this concept is simple, it is one of the hardest things for people to grasp. Many of us learned to memorize a speech and we were told that confident speakers don't need outlines. Let me ask you this — the last time you listened to a speech that was read or memorized, did you feel connected or struck by the speaker's message? Most of my students and clients will answer "no". For those who answer "yes", kudos to the speaker. To connect with your audience through a memorized or manuscript speech, you must be a very talented speaker.

When using an outline, extemporaneous speaking allows us to connect with our audience through eye contact, a conversational approach, and the ability to adapt to audience feedback. This is nearly impossible if we are reading or relaying a memorized speech. The beauty of extemporaneous speaking lies in connecting with your audience. I recently read in a Harvard Business Review article that Nancy Duarte suggests people may fall asleep during presentations, but not during conversations.

Often in my classes a student approaches me with this look of panic and describes how they have never given a speech without memorizing it. They give me multiple reasons why they are not comfortable with using an outline and practically beg me to forgive that they may have to memorize their speech. I always stand my 5' 4" ground and let them down softly. I say that this is the requirement of the class and if they don't use a proper formatted outline, they will fail.

One student stood at least seven inches taller than I, his arms the size of my thighs, with a very professional and clean look, and an extremely confident stance. As he gazed down at me giving me the reasons I mentioned in the previous paragraph, I stood there and said "Dathan, you must trust the process and trust me. In fact, I want you to write your outline and only practice the speech once. Then you have to put it down and just wing it." There was a moment I considered running out of the room. His pupils dilated, his jaw seemed clenched and he did not look happy. After an awkward silence, I said, "You can go through your life memorizing your speeches, but you have so much more to give your audience. Just do it!" At that moment Dathan had no idea that he was about to change my life as much as I may have changed his. I had never felt more confident about what I was feeling and never felt that confident stating it.

Dathan's speech was by no means perfect, but he was authentic and used the words in his well-organized outline to trigger his memory of the thought or idea he was looking to get across to his audience. He presented and revealed his authentic speaking voice. Now he could feel the audience's response to his message by engaging in eye contact by using the outline correctly. Because this was so new to him, it felt different. His "Ah-ha!" moment happened when he realized that the audience loved him authentically. He did not "have to be" the person he thought his audience wanted him to be. Bringing his voice, his personality, and his expertise authentically to the audience was exactly what they craved. Today, I am proud to receive emails and updates of his successes. Hopefully, when he reads this book, he will finally know how much he helped me!

Now that we have scratched the surface on outlines, let's dig a bit deeper into the meaning of extemporaneous speaking.

4
Investing in Your Outline

Organization Continued

Recently, I did some pro-bono work for an organization called GlamourGals. This non-profit organization promotes young women to create and lead chapters by recruiting compassionate teen volunteers to provide makeovers and manicures to senior women in assisted living facilities. During my presentation on Creating Your Pitch, I included my O.C.D Presentation Method ™. I was surprised that not one volunteer knew the three types of speeches: Manuscript, Impromptu, and Extemporaneous.

During our high school years we are encouraged to memorize our speeches.

Let's review the three types of speeches below:

Manuscript: Read from a pre-printed document or fully commit to memory

Impromptu: Off the cuff; with no prior preparation

Extemporaneous: Delivered from a well-structured outline derived from an organizational speech pattern.

This book and my curriculum are based on Extemporaneous Speech.

Let's begin to look at the process of creating an Extemporaneous speech.

While creating your outline, you must also choose an organizational speech pattern.

Picking an organizational speech pattern depends on three things: your topic, your audience, and how you want to get your message across. The following are a few examples of organizational speech patterns:

1. Topical Organizational Pattern

This pattern is mostly used for informative speeches, and might also be used for persuasive speeches. The most important thing to remember about this pattern is REPEAT, REPEAT, REPEAT.

See the full Topical Pattern Outline in Chapter 3.

2. Monroe's Motivated Sequence

The motivated sequence pattern of arrangement was developed in the mid-1930's by Alan Monroe. (4.1)

The purpose of Monroe's Motivated Sequence is to persuade your audience to change their thoughts, feelings, ideas, and/or to take an action.

I. Arouse attention
II. Demonstrate a need (Putting forward to your audience that there is a problem: an action needs to be taken and something needs to be fixed, changed, or altered)
III. Satisfy the need (Providing the solution)
IV. Visualize the results (Give your audience the perspective of projecting the outcome and satisfying the need)
V. Call for action (Give your audience tangible, immediate, and creative action)

Here's a sample outline of Monroe's Motivated Sequence:

Pattern: Monroe's Motivated Sequence
General Purpose: To Persuade
Specific Purpose: To persuade my audience to use the two main components of this Harvard Extension School Course to become a better public speaker.

I. Arouse attention: Standing in front you
    A. Person terrified public speaking
        1. Me at 20
            a. self-centered fear
            b. insecurities
            c. was painfully shy
    B. After self-taught
        1. Still something missing
    C. Not alone or not taking class

II. Demonstrate need—better communication
    A. Our world benefit
        1. More effective communicators
        2. Start in this class
        3. Stats and figures breakdowns
    B. Students enter class
        1. Fears
        2. Share breakdowns and complications
        3. Challenges with communications
    C. Leave
        1. Empowered,
            a. better listeners
            b. new techniques
            c. toolbox filled
    D. Question is How…

III. Satisfy the need—this class teaches
    A. How to overcome nerves

B. How to create working outline
C. How to connect audience
    1. Concise message
    2. Audience centered content
    3. Use non-verbals express

IV. Visualize the results—Imagine a world
    A. Use voice to share
        1. Our thoughts feelings/ideas
        2. Feel heard
        3. Overcome fear
        4. Provide clear message
        5. Reduce so much divide

V. Call for action- Take out a piece of paper
    A. Think—Share with world
    B. Write—Thesis Statement
    C. Consider—Who your audience
    D. Breathe—1st step better speaker

3. Refutative Design

This pattern resembles a debate, and begins with presenting the opposing position first. The next step is to communicate the pitfalls of the opposing claim, and then provide evidence to support the speaker's position. The conclusion is meant to drive home the speaker's argument, reinforcing the weight of the speaker's position with superiority.

4. Problem-Solution Pattern

This pattern begins with introducing the problem followed by the solution.

1. Identify the problem that is in need of a solution
2. Determine how to solve the problem.

5. Comparative Advantages Pattern

This pattern can be used most effectively when your audience is already familiar with an existing issue. Less time is spent informing the audience of the problem, and more time is spent comparing favorable solutions and alternatives. The conclusion is meant to bring focus on the specific advantages over the alternative.

Once a pattern is chosen, it is helpful to have a Cover Page for all speeches. This provides a clear and concise beginning to your speech, or at a minimum, jump starts the process of putting together a presentation.

See the example of a Cover Page below:

Name: *Helps center us and makes us accountable for our work*

Topic: *Begins the process of honing our topic down to four words or less*

Pattern: (See prior list of Organizational Patterns) *Allows us to consider what approach needs to be used in delivering our message*

General Purpose: To Persuade, To Inform, To Entertain. *This one is easy, but is important to determine whether we need to include the Elements of Persuasion or not*

Specific Purpose: *Thesis statement sets the foundation and gives us a reference point to stay on track*

Central Idea: Only used for the Topical Pattern. *This begins the honing process of choosing main points to support our Specific Purpose. This also becomes the road map for our audience and provides us with opportunities to reduce filler words by using the proper sign posts, internal reviews, and internal previews throughout.*

You may think you don't need a pattern to deliver a quick pitch, opening statement for your weekly meeting, or speech for the company party, but...what happened the last time you didn't use an organizational speech pattern? *Did you feel nervous? Did you find it hard to connect with your audience? Did you find that it fell flat? Did you think it was difficult to hold the attention of your audience? Did you say 'um' and 'so' more than a few times? Did you wish you had put more time into preparing? Did you have little or no recollection of what specific points you made after you finished?* If you answered yes to any of these, you may want to consider using a pattern.

Here are my reasons why using patterns works:

1. It reduces nerves.
2. It makes us feel organized, which increases confidence.
3. It can improve interpersonal communication by exercising the brain to present information in a logical structure rather than skip from point to point
4. It decreases the use of filler words (um, so, etc)
5. It trains our minds to think in an organized fashion, which can be extremely helpful for impromptu speaking.

Other Benefits of Using an Organizational Pattern:

The human brain is intricate. In June 2018, Arkady Konovalov and Ian Krajbich wrote "Neurocomputational Dynamics of Sequence Learning," and conducted research in which individuals learned to detect patterns in sequences of images while going through an fMRI. Summarizing from their research that "the brain is often able to learn complex structures of the environment using a very limited amount of evidence, which is crucial for model-based planning and sequential prediction." (4.2) This is to say, with enough exposure, our brain is able to piece together the puzzle or pattern. In a recent article by Ohio State University News, Konovalov said, "Humans try to detect patterns in their environment all the time because, it makes learning easier." (4.3) While this was a visual experiment, we can see that this is analogous when presenting information to a listening audience. By using a well-structured outline, your audience is more likely to remember your message. Picking the pattern that best suits your audience can help reach more members of the crowd and provide a consistent 'road map'.

Tips and tactile/tactical first steps for organizing a speech/presentation:

1. Pick a topic
2. Invest in Post-It Notes and start writing your thoughts and ideas down
3. Place the notes all over your desk
4. Find a pattern that best suits your intentions, audience, and topic

5. Begin to put the Post-It Notes in a logical order
6. Compile supportive data and research
7. Consider a few stories/anecdotes that are relatable to your topic
8. Think about your 'fire in the belly' and personal connection to the topic
9. Begin writing an outline in the proper format with *4 words or less per line*

Proper Outline Format Sample

Pattern: Topical Pattern
General Purpose: To Inform
Specific Purpose: To inform my audience about two main components of Public Speaking class at Harvard

Central Idea (main points): To inform my audience about two main components of a Public Speaking class at Harvard Extension School by sharing tools to overcome nerves and techniques to create a well-organized speech

I. Introduction
    A. (Attention Getter) Imagine—didn't fear giving speech
      1. Felt confident
      2. Well organized outline

    3. Able embrace the applause

  B. (Motivational Statement) Main components of class

    1. Enhance your career

    2. Help improve your communication

  C. (Credibility Statement) My story ...

  D. (Preview Statement) Cover two components class

    1. NERVES: What causes/tools overcome

    2. Techniques deliver organized speech

II. (1st Main Point) Nerves

  A. Science

    1. Data and numbers

    2. Studies show

    3. Amygdala

  B. Examples how to overcome

    1. Prepare

    2. Practice

    3. Power pose

III. (2nd Main Point) Strategies for creating outline

  A. How to begin

    1. Post it

    2. Research audience

    3. Thesis statement

    4. Create cover page

    5. Begin outline

B. Choose pattern
    1. Follow closely
    2. Dangers of hybrid
    3. Plug in:
        a. startling stats
        b. narrative
        c. consider using humor
C. Practice process
    1. Once with redline
    2. Second recording
    3. Time and hone
    4. Ask 'So What'

IV. Conclusion
    A. (Review Statement) We looked at
        1. Overcome nerves
        2. Format to effective outline
    B. (Motivational Statement) Next step YOURS
    C. Welcome to class
    If persuasive, then would include a call to action

We have now completed the O in OCD. Having a well-structured and organized speech is crucial for keeping your audience engaged; however, that is not the only way to connect with your audience. The frequency, WIIFM, is another hurdle that is easily tackled with time and consideration.

5

Investing in your Audience

Content: The "C" in O.C.D

In every class or session I teach, I represent the people who don't think like you! I push you and challenge you to adapt your message to the opposite side of your natural way of thinking. This seems completely counterintuitive, but it has the biggest impact in any speech. This leads us to Content!

When developing content, we want to cast a broader net in order to appeal to the different types of thinking. By stretching outside our normal mode of thought, we can reach the people who don't think like us. That is not as easy as it sounds.

How does a former truck sales person like me change the thoughts, feelings, and ideas of people from various cultures, backgrounds, ages, and experience? By being a chameleon, a strength I never knew I had. I would walk into a tow truck company in Connecticut and talk to "Joe" while he was under a truck fixing the brakes. Only minutes later, I would enter the Board Room in one of the biggest tree companies in the Northeast and pitch selling trucks worth over a half million dollars. I always considered who I was talking to and adapted my message to them individually. I never changed who I was, but I was considerate and respectful of my audience. I would walk into my own shop and spend just as much time getting to know my mechanics as I did with my sales team or the managers.

I challenge each and every person I work with to consider the following:

In a room full of people who think like you, or have the same ideas as you, I don't doubt you can effectively persuade those people. However, often your audience consists of at least one person who does not think like you or have the same ideas or feelings that you have. How do we step outside our familiar mindset to reach those audience members? This is something that doesn't come naturally.

I represent that person who sees things differently, and will push you to step outside your comfort zone. When developing your content, look at the opposite perspective, and think conversely to the common method of thoughts and feelings you comfortably identify with.

During the Professional Development Program I

teach at Harvard Extension School, I ask participants to pick one of the words below to describe themselves.

Here are the results from multicultural groups that I have worked with at Harvard:

Creative 13%	Concrete 5%
Analytical 27%	Feeler 10%
Thinker 20%	Intuitive 25%

Sample Size of: 224 Mid to Senior Level professionals

The results of asking my audience/class this question was not shocking, but the consistency is worth noting. If half or a quarter of the class considers themselves analysts or feelers, we want to consider how to approach these members of the audience because the way they take in the message will vary. We will uncover how to pique their interests or appeal to them more specifically, when we discuss Aristotle's Appeals. Additionally, the more we know about our audience and how they take in information, the more successful we will be in reaching a broader audience in its entirety. Developing content correctly will help transform your thoughts and notes into a clear, relatable message.

I call this the 'Big Shift.' Now that we have identified and taken a closer look at how we organize our thoughts and have considered the message we want to share, we need to shift the spotlight to the audience. It is no longer about us. It is about our audience and what is in it for them, otherwise known as WIIFM. It is our job to invest in getting to know the audience.

Before we deep-dive into content, I want to share how I first learned how to get to know my audience. This was not done intentionally, but through my experience selling trucks. I was forced to adapt. Each and every day I learned about various cultures, products, industries, and personalities.

I wish I could tell you I loved selling trucks, but I didn't. I did love meeting new people, seeing new manufacturing techniques, and learning about various industries. Think about everything we eat, wear, throw away, use to heat our house, or come into contact with on a daily basis. The only way that 'stuff' gets to us is by transportation, which is usually by truck. A truck consists of a cab and chassis that host the driving components to move whatever is attached to the rear axle of the truck chassis. Truck bodies are what hold the 'stuff', and often have to be spec'd out. This requires a tremendous amount of detailed specifications that must be calculated and determined in order to accommodate the various loads that trucks haul. This can range from a vanilla box, to a platform body, to an oil tank, to a refrigerated body, to a refuse body, to a dump body, and many more styles.

Quite often I would sell the vanilla box truck, but even that had interior specifications such as, tie downs, flooring options, possible insulation for refrigeration, varying types of rear doors, side door location, overall height restrictions, and the lift gates. A LOT OF DE-TAILS. Learning all of these details was crucial for me to get to know my audience at the time. The return on that investment was all the commissions I would earn from selling over 100 trucks a year. Little did I know that these practices would be exercises for 'getting to know my audiences' for my future in public speaking.

In order to spec the correct truck, I would have to learn all about the product that needed to be delivered. This included the weight, size, and packaging of the product. All trucks on the road have a gross vehicle weight (GVW) rating and this would determine not only the price, but even what kind of license someone needs to drive the truck. Picture a sixteen foot truck filled with boxes of flowers, and how much that would weigh. Then picture a sixteen foot truck filled with containers of milk, and consider the different weight capacity for each vehicle. If that sounds complicated, well it was! What does this have to do with public speaking? The people who run and operate all these companies are just as diverse as the bodies we built for their trucks, and products that filled them! It was my job to 'get to know my audience,' or it could cost me the sale of a truck and the resulting commissions.

Let's revisit the day I went into that tow company and asked "Joe" if we could chat about his trucks. He asked me to follow him into his office and have a seat. I put down my heavy bag of brochures and grabbed my note pad and pen (these were pre-laptop days). I began asking my 16 sales questions and did not skip a beat. At one point my eyes wondered above his head to the wall behind him. At first it seemed colorful with palm trees, sandy beaches, and ocean waves. Eventually, I could not focus on him answering the questions anymore. My eyes began to focus more closely on the pictures. Suddenly, I realized it was a sea of cut out magazine pictures of these gorgeous women, but something was missing…OH, IT WAS THEIR CLOTHES!!!!!

I tried desperately to ignore the rush of heat that flooded to my cheeks, the obvious look of shock across my face, along with the feeling that my eyes were popping out of my head as my chin fell to the floor. "Joe" just kept talking, so I composed myself and kept asking away. It was at that moment I learned to adapt. "Joe" treated me with the utmost respect. This was his office and I was his guest. He was never inappropriate towards me and this was not the last time I encountered a service garage or company workshop with pictures of half-naked women on the walls. (For those readers who are appalled, believe me, I can empathize, but this was the 1990's and I was 22.)

Some may feel I should have stormed out, or excused myself. Others may see this as the price to pay for success. There is no right or wrong answer, but this was my world, and I am grateful that adapting respectfully was a huge learning experience. As previously mentioned, all of our audiences are different. We will not agree with everyone's thoughts, feelings, or ideas, but If we approach our audience without considering their point of view or empathizing, we may miss the opportunity to connect or get our point across. Reacting to something different or something that may even be offensive does not have to equate to abruptness or angry reactions. I was able to empathize with someone I may not have liked or understood.

Although my next appointment was in a fancy office building, I did not feel any more comfortable. I was directed into a conference room with a glass table. Four men dressed in very expensive suits had authoritative body language and dominant nonverbal gestures. Somehow this seemed even more off-putting than the postered wall. Now it makes sense that these men were more intimidating through the eyes of an insecure introverted 22-year-old college drop-out, but I still had to adapt. Even though I may have wanted to run out of that room as well, I stayed to finish the deal.

When thinking of Content in public speaking, we need to understand who we are talking to. This is the deciding factor of how much return we will get on our investment. If we walk into a room without knowing who we are talking to, the risks are sky high that we may not make a connection. *When we don't know our audience, the risk can be even higher that we may offend or alienate them.* If we make and take the time to know our audience, we stand a better chance of connecting. This increases our chances of influencing, changing or persuading them to take an action.

How do we do this?

It is similar to putting our money in the bank. We walk into the bank knowing how much we have to invest, but we also "invest" time in getting to know who we trust with our money. Now there are always risks, but the more you put in and the higher the return, the more money you will make at the end of the day.

In public speaking, or effective communication, we gain more by investing more.

This is not a natural first thought when putting together a presentation. Why? Well, we are also tuned into WIIFM. We get so focused on our message, we often forget who is on the receiving end. Now that you are reading this book, you don't have that excuse anymore. Here are some suggestions on how to get to know your audience.

I call this ... *Walking In Your Audience's Shoes.*

1. You can ask your audience individually or collectively questions about their thoughts, feelings, or ideas about your topic.
2. You can send out a survey prior to your speaking engagement.

3. You can ask the person who invited you to speak about the individuals, the company, and the culture of the organization.

4. You can find out some of the names of your audience (stalking is not acceptable, but why not learn as much as you can about your audience) and Google them or find them on LinkedIn.

5. You should research people who work there by logging onto the company website, which is available to everyone.

6. If there is an event before you present, you can ask to attend and meet your audience. Spend time getting to know them in an informal setting. This eliminates the unfamiliar aspect, and gives you smiles in the audience.

7. You can walk around and meet people in the audience the day of the event. Having small talk is invaluable for finding out things you have in common with some of the audience. This establishes a connection.

8. If the meeting is with familiar colleagues, send out a few questions prior to the meeting to learn more about the thoughts, feelings, and/or ideas of your audience.

One small gift I give to all my students and clients is a small keychain with a shoe attached. My message along with this gift is always to place this shoe at the top of your outline to remind you to 'walk in your audience's shoes.'

6
Investing in the Impact of Story Telling

Content Continued

My most impactful moment of 'getting to know my audience' happened during a workshop I lead for the Survivors Voice Program. This program was built to empower Rwandan genocide survivors and provide training to help survivors find their voice. Our workshop was not only to prepare them to participate in panel discussions and other forums as advocates, but to strengthen the healing process. This group of men and woman gathered at the Harvard Law School in 2015 to celebrate the launch of this program. A colleague offered me a volunteer opportunity to present to this group on public speaking and finding a voice.

I diligently prepared my outline and even practiced multiple times in front of my husband. I received an invitation from the host to attend the cocktail reception the night before and I am embarrassed to admit I debated going. It was a frigid February evening, I had a young child at home, and parking can be impossible at the Law School with snow as high as the parking meters. That night, I was made aware of how meaningless those thoughts were, and I still wince when I think of how foolish I was in that moment.

Walking into the cocktail reception that night, there was an atmosphere that felt incredibly different from anything I had experienced before. The colors, the smiles, and the level of energy in the room were palpable. There were beautiful and delightful women who greeted me with hugs. The men had heartfelt expressions and they had this amazing way of saying hello, giving me a true sense that they were glad to meet me. The vibrant colors they were wearing consisted of layered silk with hues of red, yellow, orange, purple, fushia, blue, and green that livened the dull, brown walls. In addition, their scarves were textured with various patterns. The night felt unique and special.

About an hour after I arrived, a woman began introducing some of the people I had just met. It was at that moment my world and my approach to my workshop changed. I began to hear stories of terror and survival. I began to 'get to know my audience.' My heart sank so deeply into my chest and I wanted to immediately apologize for even considering not attending this event. It was difficult to understand how these survivors had experienced such horrendous things, yet could exude such warmth and love. At that moment, I felt I was not worthy enough to be in a room filled with such courage, strength, and dignity.

That night, I went home and started my outline from scratch. This was not a classroom of students attending Harvard Extension School, this was not a company in Boston asking me to provide public-speaking tips, and this was not a coaching session. I needed to customize this workshop as best I could to guide these amazing survivors. To this day I wish I could do it again having had more experience but, I did the best I could and poured out my heart.

Never give up the opportunity to get to know your audience. The simplest question can bring the biggest return on your investment. When we dive into persuasion, this can save lots of time and add a huge amount of empathy and credibility to your presentation. Would you give your money to a bank you didn't know or didn't have a relationship with? *Would you give your money to a bank that did not tell you the interest rate of return?* We should apply these same principals to the way we develop our content to be audience-centered, as opposed to self-centered.

Always have a goal for your speeches or presentations, however, remember that if that goal is only self-centered, you may miss the mark. Many speaking engagements are not like my class where we can discuss the most impactful speeches and why those work and connect. We don't have the opportunity to ask our audience, *'Are you going to take that action? Did I change your minds? Do you now believe in this? Did I change your thoughts about that?'* However, one way to incorporate and connect with our audience is through a story.

Following is some background and some comments from classes about the most impactful speeches:

My students were asked to give a five minute extemporaneous informative speech from an outline in the form of a Topical Pattern. Following the speeches, we asked some of the students to pick their favorite speech of the 19 presented. Here are some of their choices and their reasoning behind them. I should mention that these speeches were purely informative, as we had not even addressed persuasion yet.

1. She was incredibly compassionate and the topic was super memorable.
2. Her subject was emotional. She shared her own experience/story and I could see how much she was passionate about the topic.
3. ...because it was also a heartbreaking speech, and I could see that it impacted her as well while she was sharing her story.
4. He did a great job providing the right depth

of information while also keeping the topic interesting.

5. ...his passion for the subject came through in his content.

6. ...his sheer level of energy and enthusiasm that he maintained throughout.

7. I also really appreciated that the story she shared as the connection to her topic was so personal.

8. He did a great job with his pace, his clarity and his content. He knew his audience...

9. Her seemingly easy graceful presentation, content, delivery, takeaway.

10. The way she told her story was really impressive.

These comments were from the very first formal speech required and given by students in my 'Fundamentals of Public Speaking' course. Notice when asked what was most memorable, they all refer to contextual and emotional aspects of the speech that related back to their own personal interest.

The Impact of storytelling: The Golden Nugget of a Successful Speech

A story or anecdote is one way to tap into your audience's

emotions and connect on a higher level. We all have previous experiences that are filed away in our brain. These experiences can easily be brought to the forefront when triggered by a memory. I don't profess to be a scientist, so here is the laymen's version: If we see, hear, smell, taste, or feel something that our brain senses or attaches to a memory, we can anticipate intentions and goals of others through our mirror neurons. Hence through the effects of sharing a story, your chances increase of tapping into your audience's emotions if they ever experienced similar feelings, thoughts or experiences. Stories are one of the reasons our species evolved to exist the way we do today. Our ancestors connected and protected through storytelling from the beginning of our existence. We often forget that if we share a story with our audience, we are proving to them we care enough about them to give them something unique about us. David JP Phillips in his TEDxStockholm, "The Magical Science of Storytelling" provides heartfelt and powerful examples of how storytelling also provides our brain the opportunity to induce hormones that enhance the connection with your audience. (6.1) My students are required to watch this video.

At times, I am still insecure, shy, and filled with self-doubt. What helps me thrive as an instructor, coach, and speaker, is that I show my audience I care about them. I do the work, make the investment, and spend tireless hours tailoring my message to my audience to the best of my ability.

My mentor and colleague, Marjorie North, often says in her Fundamentals of Public Speaking course that, "Our audience does not separate the message from the speaker." That can help or hurt us. If we take time to 'walk in our audience's shoes,' we stand a better chance of connecting and showing our audience we have invested in them. Think about customer service, and how that effects where you make your investment. Would you give someone your hard earned dollars if you didn't like them? If you thought they had not considered your thoughts, feelings, or ideas? *If you were investing for your retirement, a child's education, a big risk, or quick, turn-around investment—but, your advisor never asked what was driving your decision, or what your personal financial preferences were, how could they possibly direct you to the most appropriate investment of your dollars that would be right for you? Would you trust them with your investment?*

Let's consider the viewpoint of the bank. How exactly are they going to 'persuade' you to give them your money? If they had taken my course or heard one of my seminars, hopefully they would depend on Aristotle and his Argument of the 3 Appeals.

Greek philosopher Aristotle argued that in order to persuade an audience, the speaker should appeal to the logic and emotions of the audience, while earning credibility. "According to Aristotle, and generations of scholars and practitioners who followed him, you can build an effective persuasive speech with any one or a combination of these proofs, termed *logos, pathos,* and *ethos.* The best speeches generally make use of all three proofs." (6.2) Layering the appeals throughout a persuasive presentation can be extremely effective, and if done correctly builds confidence and a connection with an audience.

I persuaded most of my customers to purchase a truck or replace their fleet of trucks. I can honestly say, I had no clue any of these appeals existed prior to taking the exact class that I now teach at Harvard Extension School. It was during that class in 2005 that a huge lightbulb went off in my head. There was a more organized, formal and calculated approach to something I spent 14 years doing already. This was a huge 'ah-ha' moment. Many others shared that same revelation after my 'Power of Persuasion' lesson.

Logos: Logical Appeal

We think of the Latin root 'Logos' to mean logic. Aristotle gave this appeal more meaning than flow and order of words. The appeal must tap into thinking and the audience's approach to logic. Here are the key elements to consider when appealing to a person's logic:

1. Incorporating counter arguments or anticipating pushback

2. Establishing common ground
3. Including pre-empt objections
4. Presenting a well-structured and easy to follow argument
5. Including Creative refutation draws the audience in

My classes require the students to give at least one persuasive speech. I can attest it takes multiple attempts for students to grasp the many elements of Logos. However, once they hear or listen to a fellow speaker in class establish common ground among a class of various ages, culture and life experience, or pre-empt the audience's objections in a speech, the light bulb goes on. This goes back to wearing a new lens and looking beyond our own thoughts, feelings, and opinions. If we don't consider the audience's thoughts, feelings, and ideas, we will never know our chances of persuasion.

The appeal of logic also ties into the "O" in OCD Presentation Method ™. The goal that comes up most for clients and students is how to be more concise and direct in their message. One of my many words of advice is to "practice, hone, practice, hone, but not alone". This is a way to step outside of your own personal view and "walk in the audiences shoes". Logos also keeps the focus on maintaining a clear and concise message. As a result, the audience remembers your message.

All of these appeals should be layered throughout the speech. As you read through the rest of the Appeals, notice which ones may overlap. Often one approach can check the box for all three.

Pathos: Emotional Impact

Pathos is the emotion you elicit from your audience by sharing stories, startling statistics, facts or figures. Companies spend billions of dollars on marketing to figure out the direct way to your heart and wallet. Doing this in a speech goes back to the power of story-telling, and investing in 'who you are persuading' by providing relatable research to your audience.

The way I explain this appeal to my students is by asking them to recall my story of being insecure and terrified to speak in public. Many people can relate on some level to the fear of getting up in front of a sea of eyes. During that story, I reveal my 'fire in the belly', and why I have made it my life mission to help people overcome their own fears, or assist them in reaching their goals through effective communication. This personal story demonstrates the 'what is' (fear of public speaking) versus 'what can be' (overcoming the fear of public speaking). I am also acknowledging the feelings and values of my audience. A story that taps into the senses and uses imagery has the power to move an audience emotionally.

Ethos: Credibility

The most common question about credibility is how to balance coming off as a braggart versus not sharing enough to earn credibility. My immediate answer is "it's easier to maintain credibility than to have to regain credibility". Credibility is not authority and serves a connection between two people. You can be well-liked and very sociable and still not be thought of as an expert. Credibility is earned over time and during a speech it's important to layer your expertise. This can come in many different forms, such as stories or sharing your experience, knowledge, and competence. Another means of earning credibility is using statistics, quotes, and facts. All of this still falls under the umbrella of 'getting to know your audience'. Using stories, facts, figures, and statistics are crucial in the success of tapping into this appeal. However, they all must be relatable to your topic and your audience.

Below are comments from students regarding incorporating Logos, Ethos and Pathos...

There is an art to storytelling...when there is emotion in a story, it is far more likely to pull me in and be interesting.

I agree that building a "bank of stories" is important to one's success in their personal or business life.....

The versatile nature of storytelling will help the information stay with the audience and makes the communication memorable.

Stories have the power of making information palatable, unlike sharing some scientific facts or data.

Overall, being able to incorporate stories throughout a presentation is a skill that is essential

…the importance of Ethos and in particular how a loss of credibility will quickly result in an audience becoming disengaged and any further appeal to logic (Logos) will be harder to achieve

Going into my speech, I really do feel that the "fire in the belly" in regard to my dog, and the love that I have for her, DID help me stay calm and assisted me with staying focused. There was so much that I wanted to share, so many ideas that I wanted to get out, but all I could hear was Jill's voice saying, "less is more" and that was able to keep me focused on my topic.

Interestingly, as I continually have to give persuasive speeches at my workplace, with every speech I now strategize the speech on how to use Logos, Ethos, Pathos for maximum effect.

Using the appeals to persuade an audience can be extremely effective. Each one functions independently, but can overlap with another. Always make sure to include all three, but know including one may check the box for the others.

I must add the one final note about Content. Getting to know your audience results in experience, knowledge, and often making mistakes. Ironically, I learned this early on in my career. Here are a few examples:

Selling trucks in NY and the five boroughs, I had the chance to engage with clients who came from various ethical, moral, and cultural backgrounds. I had many embarrassing moments learning to navigate some of these diversities at a very young age. I learned not to extend a hand to those who could not return the handshake due to religious reasons. I learned how to receive and read a business card when it was created to hold more meaning than letters just printed on a business card. Each letter, symbol, and character was strategically placed, and if ignored or overlooked would be a direct insult to the person handing it out. I also learned the importance of 'small talk.' I learned which customers negotiated after, before, or during coffee, lunch, or tea. Sometimes it shocked me how yelling could all be part of the sport of negotiation, and then once it was over, I had a customer for life!

The most impactful experience I had still plays in my head. Prior to Daimler Benz purchasing Freightliner, Mercedes Benz commercial trucks were sold in the US. During one of my earlier cold-calling days in the meat market, I walked by one of the open garage doors and spoke with the owner of a company. When I handed the gentlemen the card, he took a minute to look at the card. The conversation began with smiles and what I thought was a nice start to the process. As I handed him my card, his facial expression changed to a rigid frown. Then he ripped the corner of my business card off, and abruptly handed it back. With fury in his eyes and pursed lips, he said, "I will never buy a truck from a German company." I was stunned and shocked and at first I didn't understand what he did to my card. I then realized that he had ripped off the Mercedes Benz logo. It wasn't until 16 years later when I had the chance to travel to Poland and visit Auschwitz and Birkenau that I fully understood the emotion behind why he gave me back my card. All of these exchanges and interactions helped me understand and respect ethical, moral, and cultural differences at an early age. I do my best to always respect and consider who my audience is and where they come from.

Let's now take our well-structured, organized, and audience-centered message and convey it with confidence by using our natural delivery style.

7
Investing in your Non-Verbal Communication

Delivery: The "D" in O.C.D

What is so important about how we stand, or use our hands, or whether or not we look at our audience? Why does this always come up around public speaking? Why is this a crucial and regular point in effective communication?

One reason is that our audience is watching us, and therefore we need to appear confident in delivering our message. If we don't appear confident, will they doubt us or stop listening to us? We need to build our credibility with body language that matches the message we are delivering. It's important to note that, humans take in 40 bits of information per second consciously, and 11 million bits of information per second subconsciously. (7.1) So even if our audience thinks we are great, they are still subconsciously responding to non-verbal messages, which can negatively impact our connection with the audience.

Before each class, session, or professional development course I teach, I ask one simple question: What are the three things you want to most improve about your public speaking? At least one of the responses falls under the category of Delivery.

Here are the most common answers that specifically relate to our non-verbal communication:
- Improve eye contact with my audience
- Increase or reduce gestures
- Hide my random nervous hand movements
- Slow down
- Eliminate filler words

Here are the most common goals by the end of my semester:
- Reduce weight shifting or what I call 'the dance'
- Stop random movement
- Use more gestures
- Reduce filler words
- Use the 'Power of Pause'
- Stop fidgeting
- Stop self-touch (hair, glasses, sleeves, wedding ring)
- Reduce bobbing head while trying to have eye contact

- Do not have a death grip on the lectern
- Stop pointing

Before any of my students receive the video of their speech, I share that watching their recorded speeches will reveal at least one thing they never realized they did while presenting. The one student who challenged me, and said this would not happen, humbly returned to the next class with a full admission that, he never realized he used the filler word "um" so many times.

We are self-centered beings so intent on sharing our message that we don't often recognize HOW we are delivering our message.

If you take only one thing away from reading this book let it be this: DON'T wait to work on your delivery skills until the moment of your speech. When presenting, you want to focus on improving no more than TWO things. Any more than two can be problematic. A highly accomplished client of mine gave a speech for a well-known company that hosts presentations. As she went on stage, the speaking coach instructed, 'Don't forget to slow down.' Those words rang through her head throughout the entire speech, and rather than enjoying the exchange of information with the audience, she slowed down so much that it never quite felt comfortable, and she never got into her natural rhythm. This ties into the approach of being authentic.

When it comes to using our non-verbals to enhance our message, our audience will trust their eyes more than their ears. The McGurk Effect is an auditory illusion where a voice articulating a consonant is dubbed with a face articulating another consonant. (7.2) In BBC's Horizon Clip, Professor Lawrence Rosenblum explains that in the McGurk Effect illusion "what we see overrides what we hear. So the mouth movements we see as we look at a face can actually influence what we believe we're hearing. If we close our eyes, we actually hear the sound as it is. If we open our eyes, we actually see how the mouth movement can influence what we are hearing." (7.3) You may recognize the voice speech alone but, after dubbing the voice speech with a conflicting visual, your brain recognizes the voice speech as something different. For example, in the BBC clip, "ba" is being dubbed over the visual mouth movements of "fa". With only audio, you hear "ba". With audio and the divergent visual, you hear "fa". From a public speaking perspective, this effect confirms that our brain trusts our eyes more than our ears. So when presenting our non-verbals, being consistent with your language prevents your audience from becoming confused and lowers the risk of losing your audience's attention.

The audience can sense when you have too much on your mind, so don't overfill it with things you want to change while presenting. You have the constant opportunity to work on your communication skills and become aware of your communication style.

Each and every day you have the chance to engage with others and practice non-verbals. Whether standing at the grocery store or waiting to tee off at the golf course, why not focus on your posture, eye contact, and gestures? *When you stand for long periods of time, notice if you are shifting your weight from one leg to another. Do you hold eye contact with your colleagues, or do you tend to look down, or out the window? Do you have your hands in your pockets a lot, or do you immediately go to the 'spider in the mirror' gesture to appear confident?*

If you become more self-aware during your daily communication, it will become more natural when you are on stage. I have trained my body to revert to a confident posture, constantly striving to look at my audience in its entirety, and using my natural gestures and body language to emphasize my points or connect with my audience.

This did not happen overnight. I practice what I preach with daily consistency. The stakes are high for me. My students are watching every teaching moment, and wondering if I am going to say 'um', shift my weight, or forget to look at the audience. I still don't have it down perfectly and that allows me to be an example that this process is about progress, not perfection. Thankfully, our audiences are just as self-centered as we are, and are mostly tapped into their own WIIFM (What's In It For Me), and not focusing on our gestures or posture every second. However, they are taking in your message, consciously and subconsciously, and the more aware and confident we are in our delivery, the more we can focus on establishing a connection with our audience.

A few years ago I found out that one reason I had a bad back was because one leg is a bit shorter than the other. However, in practicing what I preach, I am constantly checking my posture when at cocktail parties, waiting for the dog to do her business, watching my son at his baseball games, talking to colleagues at the elevator, or chatting with students after class. I correct my posture to have my weight equally distributed between my feet, shoulder-width apart and, as a result, have trained my body to automatically go into the 'proper posture' mode whenever I am presenting. Proper posture mode and not slouching will appear less distracting and more confident.

When I was 25 years old, I realized I was not holding eye contact. I was so intimidated, I often looked down or away from clients. During this time, I was traveling around the US with other owners of truck dealerships, and had to present my ideas to, or answer questions from, a group of 20 people, who had decades more experience than I had. I was there representing my family's business and had to act, sound, and articulate in a confident manner. That is when I began working on holding eye contact. In order to feel more comfortable, I started with close friends and colleagues. I slowly chipped away and began to feel that I was just as important as the person I was talking to, and realized that if I wanted to be heard, I needed to connect through eye contact. This took a long time and I had many set-backs. If I had just broken up with a boyfriend, lost a truck deal, and felt slightly 'less than,' it was more difficult. However, the more I held eye contact, the more I felt heard and the more I spoke up, resulting in a confirmation of connection.

It was right around this time that I began to join industry associations to market our dealership and the trucks we sold. I would attend at least one meeting a week with groups like the Connecticut Groundskeepers Association, and the New York State Turf and Landscape Association. I also attended meetings and events of local organizations for electricians, plumbers, and many more. I was always one of very few women in the room, and was charged with introducing myself and the company and giving some background on my product. This was extremely difficult and horrifying for me! It was very unusual for a woman to be selling trucks. I certainly did not blend in, but the more I became comfortable in my own skin, the easier it became for me.

I am eternally grateful for the kind, seasoned professionals who encouraged and supported me and my efforts. Many of them had daughters who had no interest in getting into their business, and they gained a high level of respect for me. It was not until many years later that I began to focus on posture, gestures, and vocal variety. Now, it is second nature.

It was also around this time in my career that I attended many sessions at our annual National Industry Convention, ATD (American Truck Dealer) Association. It was at one ATD session, that I heard the phrase that rings true for me regarding Delivery:

"Inspect, What You Expect."

Why wouldn't we 'inspect what we expect' before we deliver a speech to an audience? When running a department or team, we set high expectations and actionable goals. Without crossing the line into 'micro-managing,' it is crucial to supply our teams with the proper tools to execute tasks. We arm our teams with psychological testing, team building events, weekly/monthly meetings, inventory control, analytics, consumer analysis, yearly reviews, bonuses, quarterly reports, accountability scales, and multiple opportunities laying out expectations from the owners, board members, clients, vendors, and executive board.

Rather than focus on our delivery style, we either wing it, assuming that if we don't see our flaws, neither will our audience, or we ignore our delivery style altogether. Most people don't inspect their delivery style because it's simply uneasy to look at our own flaws. If we ignore them, we don't have to do the work to fix them. However, as the book title asserts, we need to "re-invest in your rhetoric."

Here are some ways to "inspect what you expect":

Become aware of how long and how often you hold eye contact during your daily interactions.
- As you become comfortable holding eye contact in smaller groups, begin to spread your eye contact within larger groups. It is easier to consider the audience as a group of individuals, rather than a sea of eyes. Think about our ancestors and how they reacted to a sea of eyes approaching their village. Their fight or flight reaction is directly related to the evolution of

our society. We can tell our amygdala that we are not in impending danger, our audience is not the enemy.

- Be sure your eye contact is culturally appropriate and aligned with your audience's background.

Take notice of your posture as you stand. If you practice holding your weight evenly distributed between your two feet at shoulder width apart, you are more likely to adopt this posture when you are presenting.

- Practice standing the same way you want to stand while presenting during the regular course of your day.
- Record yourself and make sure you are not shifting your weight, swaying or 'doing the dance.'

Practice keeping your hands at rest. Most people don't practice this or even take notice of their hands. Usually our hands are holding a pen, a phone, a pad, or otherwise occupied. However when we stand on stage, we often feel as though we have two awkward extensions of your arms that have no apparent purpose, other than to be distracting and in the way. Don't let that happen! Practice 'hands at rest' whenever you are having a conversation. Next time you are at a cocktail party, put your drink down, hold your hands in a comfortable position at your side, or loosely clasped at your belly button, and feel that awkwardness. Better it happen when others are under the influence at a party, rather than serve as a distraction during a presentation on stage.

Practice keeping your gestures natural. Avoid gestures that may trigger your audience, such as pointing or hiding your hands in your pockets. If you have a lot of nervous energy, let your hands be a release of that tension. Either refer to the recording you did with me in class, or record yourself giving a brief speech.

- Notice if your hands gesture naturally or not. Do not force or practice gestures, as they can appear unnatural and awkward to the audience.

Use the lectern as the tool it is intended to be; a place to put your outline, presentation remote, or prop. Do not lean on the lectern, hold on to it with a death grip, or bang on it as the microphone may pick up the sound and negatively affect the audio.

Keep your movements intentional and purposeful. Nothing is more distracting during a presentation than a speaker doing a mad dash from one end of the stage to the other. Here are two suggestions regarding movement on stage:

- If you are inclined to move during a speech, start in the middle and move to one side, pause and make a point. Then move back to the center, pause and make a point, and then go to the

65

other side and repeat. Treat all sides of the room equally.

- When trying purposeful movement, maintain an ARC of open body language to the audience in its entirety, making sure not to give any members of the audience the 'cold shoulder.' One slight turn of the body could be construed as 'giving the audience your back'. This may not register consciously, but subconsciously you may have just given them permission to tune out or check their phone.

Be mindful of your overall energy as it is extremely relevant. Low energy can be an audience killer, while too much energy can seem overwhelming or distracting. How your energy level is perceived depends on your delivery style, the topic at hand, and your audience. The effectiveness of your energy level depends on knowing your audience, understanding their level of enthusiasm, and bringing your own appropriate level of excitement to the presentation. If you are passionate and excited, the audience will feel that passion and excitement as well.

Use your vocal variety as it is an important part of your delivery. Most of us don't pay attention to our natural range in pitch, intensity, rate, and rhythm when we talk. Now, through a new lens, I am asking you to not only become familiar with your voice, but to use vocal variety when delivering a speech. Let your voice be a tool to connect with your audience. Let it be the vehicle to drive points home, make numbers impactful, and give your experience and expertise the merit it deserves.

- Incorporate a variety in pitch and intensity by using dialogue
- Soften your volume to draw the audience in and place emphasis
- Use the 'Power of Pause' to make your words impactful while, giving the audience time to absorb your message. Get comfortable with silence.

All of this takes time, experience, and practice. It has taken me many years to accept and understand my natural communication style. Through this process, I have become aware of my strengths and weaknesses. I continue to stay aware of what needs improvement and what I do well. All of this changes with time, age, and experiences, and it will work the same way for you as you progress and improve your public speaking.

Here's a quick anecdote about identifying my voice:

At the age of 32, I arrived at Harvard Extension school. I was still quite shy and had to lick my wounds after leaving my family business. During many classes and group meetings with students, I found myself not using my voice. After taking Marjorie North's classes, I began to appreciate my unique delivery style. It was still far from perfect, and once I realized that, although perfection isn't possible, progress is, if you work at it.

I kept chipping away. I stepped way outside my comfort zone on multiple occasions. I realized that there is no perfection, only progress. Only we decide how we feel after presenting. It is not like an Olympic competition. There is no judge holding up a scorecard with a number at the end of our speeches. It is up to you, as the speaker, to strive for maximum impact with every speech. It is up to you to celebrate your strengths and continue to look for areas to improve. The tools and techniques I mention in this book are here for you. We can reach for them at any time. And know that as you become more polished and comfortable, the tools will have different and more advanced meaning.

Less than a year ago, I was finally at a point in my career where I felt comfortable and confident using my voice every day to change lives when I experienced a set-back. I needed surgery for a deviated septum and nasal bone spur. The surgery produced a nasal sound to my voice, although some would say it was something only I noticed.

As I have slowly accepted my new voice, I encourage all my students to accept theirs as they use it as a tool to connect with their audience. The lesson here is that we all have to come to terms with various challenges and we should view that challenge as a strength rather than seeing it as a weakness.

Here are some goals I would like to leave you with:
- organize your message clearly and concisely
- invest in what you want to say...
- invest in how to capitalize on what goes on beyond the written or spoken word; ie, connecting with your audience using body language.
- be aware that your voice and how you use your hands can enhance your connection with your audience.
- become comfortable with your natural tools and body language to convey your message to effectively communicate with your audience.

If you practice using these new 'investments' and skills in everyday life, you will be successful at it becoming natural for you and you will succeed in 'reinvesting in your rhetoric'.

8
Reinvesting in YOU

Your Official Pocket Guide to Investing in Your Rhetoric

"OCD Presentation Method"

Now you have the foundation of OCD, and you have made an investment in your rhetoric by taking the time to read this book. Hopefully, you have also learned new ways to 'get to know your audience' and consider their thoughts, feelings, and ideas while persuading them to either change an existing view or influencing them to take an action.

The importance of taking time to assess your baseline of communication provides an appreciation for what you do well, and areas for improvement. Work on those areas of improvement before you step on stage. You will be more relaxed with proper planning and organizing your outline, and you can focus on excelling in the areas that you do well. If you have strong story-telling skills and realize that sharing your personal experiences evokes your vocal variety, concentrate on those skills.

At the same time, work on keeping your hands at rest, 'standing your ground' by having confident posture, releasing your nervous energy by using non-verbal cues and by tapping into your senses by using descriptive language to make complicated concepts easier to understand. These may be details you never considered before reading this book.

I promise that if you take the time to work at the steps outlined throughout this book, you will improve your public speaking with new-found confidence. What you get out of this book will depend on what you put into it.

In conclusion, I want to share some of the wonderful elements of communication I learned from my students.

1. Take risks, and if you believe in something, don't quit or hold back. 'Unleash the beast' and tap into the 'fire in the belly.' Go for it!

2. Listening and be empathetic...the magic recipe to effective communication.

3. Worrying about your audience is a good thing. It indicates you are willing to invest in them.

4. Learning how to use the 'power of pause' can be very effective.

5. Leaving yourself a voice messages can help

with understanding how you use your voice naturally.

6. Using an outline is the key ingredient in becoming more concise and more organized.
7. A call to action needs to be immediate, creative, and memorable.
8. Proper planning prevents poor performance.
9. Fantasize about using glue on your shoes to stand in one place if you 'do the dance.'

You now know the key ingredients to becoming a better presenter; use them wisely and allow them to become your own...you can do it! I wish you much success!

Stay tuned for my next book on leadership communication and how to be a better audience.

One final note, I would be remiss if I did not mention this book was completed during the Coronavirus outbreak. We have all been forced to shift to a virtual world of communication. It seemed appropriate to add some helpful hints about converting to an online communication platform. Please note a few suggestions below:

1. Always invest just as much time and energy into your virtual presence and audience as you would in an in-person presentation.
2. Despite our new greeting, "you are muted,"

learning and adjusting to new technology takes time and patience.

3. Secure appropriate lighting, framing, appearance, and posture.

4. Set the culture of any communication online early on to allow for others to voice their thoughts, ideas, and opinions.

5. Give your virtual presence depth and texture using your voice and non-verbals.

6. Just because the 'mute' button is on, that does not mean the camera is off!

7. Do your best to maintain eye contact with the camera.

8. Invest in your set up by checking your audio and your visual presence well before your meeting.

Bibliography

Chapter 2

2.1 Simons, T. (1998). *Scared Speechless: Understanding And Conquering Stage Fright.* Presentations, 12(9), 39-46. Retrieved from http://search.proquest.com.ezp-prod1.hul.harvard.edu/docview/224631763?accountid=11311

Chapter 4

4.1 Monroe, A.H. (1935) *Principles And Types Of Speech.* Chicago, IL: Scott Foresman.

4.2 Konovalov, A., & Krajbich, I. (2018). *Neurocomputational Dynamics of Sequence Learning.* Neuron, 98(6), 1282-1293.e4.

4.3 Grabmeier, J. (2018, July 10). *This Is Your Brain Detecting Patterns.* Retrieved from https://news.osu.edu/this-is-your-brain-detecting-patterns/

Chapter 6

6.1 TEDx Talks. (2017, March). *The Magical Science Of Storytelling | David JP Phillips | TEDxStockholm*. [Video File] Retrieved from https://youtu.be/Nj-hdQMa3uA

6.2 O'Hair, D., Stewart, R. A., & Rubenstein, H. (2012). *A Speaker's Guidebook*. New York, NY: Bedford/St. Martins.

Chapter 7

7.1 Morgan, N. (2014). Power cues : *The Subtle Science Of Leading Groups, Persuading Others, And Maximizing Your Personal Impact*. Boston, Massachusetts: Harvard Business Review Press.

7.2 Mcgurk, H. & Macdonald J. (1976). *Hearing Lips And Seeing Voices*. Nature, 264(5588), 746-748.

7.3 BBC. (2010, November). *Try This Bizarre Audio Illusion*—BBC. [Video File] Retrieved from https://youtu.be/G-lN8vWm3m0

About the Author

Jill Slye teaches multiple courses and professional development programs on Public Speaking, Professional Presenting, and Leadership Communication at Harvard University Extension School. She recently accepted a position teaching at the Harvard School of Dental Medicine, offering the MMSc students a year long course on Leadership Communication. Her courses attract diverse people from around the globe. Additionally, she owns her own coaching company and has worked with people from the various schools at Harvard. Outside of Harvard, her clients consist of employees and executives from marketing firms, hospitals, technology companies, and non-profit organizations. Her programs focus on techniques to improve public speaking and effective communication skills. Jill's twenty-nine years of business experience in sales, management, and marketing provide the basis for her understanding of her audience and enhance her ability to relate to her clients and students.